# Inspiration vs. Discipline

## An owner's guide to winning on their Business Journey

By Cherry-Ann Carmelia Craigwell

## About the Author

Cherry-Ann Craigwell is a consultant on commerce and business development. She has 27 years experience in Customer Service, Business and Process Development, Strategic Management and Business Culture Management. Her experience has shown there is the need for Small and Medium Enterprises to adopt fundamental practices to support their sustainability and competitiveness in the environment. Her passion for building business has purposed her to provide operational and strategy coaching services to Sole Traders and Small and Medium Sized Enterprises.

Other books written by the author –

> The Building Ideas Guide Handbook

> Utility Solutions for Businesses – USB for Small and Medium Enterprises

> Transition & Recovery – An SME Roadmap for Effective Strategy

Inspiration vs. Discipline – An Owner's Guide to winning on their Business Journey, Copyright © 2021 by Cherry-Ann Carmelia Craigwell. All rights reserved. Printed in the United States of America. No part of this book may be reproduced in any manner whatsoever without permission except in the case of brief quotation embodied in critical articles and reviews.

ISBN 9798411862416

# Table of Contents

Introduction ............................................................................ 4
The Tortoise and the Hare ..................................................... 5
Characterization ..................................................................... 7
    The Tortoise – The Manager ............................................... 7
    The Hare – The Hustler ....................................................... 9
The Race – The Business Journey ........................................ 11
    Business Journey - Phases ................................................ 13
    Trust .................................................................................. 15
    Self-Sufficiency ................................................................. 16
    Innovation and Action ...................................................... 16
    Enterprising ...................................................................... 17
    Distinction ........................................................................ 17
    Cohesiveness .................................................................... 18
    Commitment .................................................................... 18
    Continuity ......................................................................... 19
Story Analysis ....................................................................... 20
    The Callout ....................................................................... 20
    The Response ................................................................... 22
    Ready, Set, Go! ................................................................. 24
    The Finish ......................................................................... 27
Summary ............................................................................... 29

# Introduction

The characteristics of Inspiration and Discipline can be compared to the personalities of the Hustler and the Manager.

The Hustler using inspiration focuses on creating immediate opportunities that are accessible through network relationships, readily available resources and market needs.

While, the Manager with discipline concentrates on the building of processes, policies, maintenance and accountability for achieving set goals.

The balanced application of Inspiration and Discipline, for the leading of the business by the owner is important for the success of it.

In the following pages, we will explore the disadvantages of these two skills if they are employed by themselves and the advantages of when they work together. We will also consider how they can be harnessed in the operations of the business at different stages of the business journey to bring about success.

## The Tortoise and the Hare

The tale of the tortoise and the hare is a popular English tale. We will be using this well known story to learn, understand and compare the personalities of a Hustler and a Manager.

Please see excerpt taken from the Library of Congress – Aesop Tales

A Hare was making fun of the Tortoise one day for being so slow.

"Do you ever get anywhere?" he asked with a mocking laugh.

"Yes," replied the Tortoise, "and I get there sooner than you think. I'll run you a race and prove it."

The Hare was much amused at the idea of running a race with the Tortoise, but for the fun of the thing he agreed. So the Fox, who had consented to act as judge, marked the distance and started the runners off.

The Hare was soon far out of sight, and to make the Tortoise feel very deeply how ridiculous it was for him to try a race with a Hare, he lay down beside the course to take a nap until the Tortoise should catch up.

The Tortoise meanwhile kept going slowly but steadily, and, after a time, passed the place where the Hare was sleeping.

But the Hare slept on very peacefully; and when at last he did wake up, the Tortoise was near the goal.

The Hare now ran his swiftest, but he could not overtake the Tortoise in time.

"Inspiration helps you start; Discipline helps you finish. You need both to win"

- Cherry-Ann Craigwell

http://read.gov/aesop/025.html

# Characterization

The story about the Tortoise and the Hare is a simple one of a race that was ensued between two very different animals completing the same course. We will examine the personalities of the Manager and the Hustler as they experience the journey (race) of business ownership.

The strengths and weaknesses of each animal will be considered, and how it added value or hindered their success in the race, and this will be compared to the efforts of the Manager and the Hustler on their business journey.

## The Tortoise – The Manager

The tortoise is a reptile with a huge shell which is used as protection against the elements of danger. Its movements are slow and methodical and it steadily completes its course of action using little energy therefore allowing it to be constant in its effort.

The tortoise, uses it shell as protection from its predators and it do not hunt, for it is an herbivore, hence it is not necessary for the tortoise to move quickly, but to comfortably stay secure and safe while quietly moving through its life journey.

Its behavior and personality can be likened to that of a manager, where this personality seeks to secure and safely guide the business, by ensuring maintenance and accountability processes are instilled and practiced.

Like the shell of the Tortoise, the responsibilities of the business can be comfortably carried and adopted by the manager personality. There is the need for the manager to feel safe and protected, and this personality practices the different factors that are necessary in the proper maintenance for the safety of the business. It steadily implements the right policies, processes and practices in order to ensure operation stability for the success of set objectives.

It creates a comfort space so that it can be excellent in its functions as the little wins are important for its continued agreeable existence.

The habit of establishing small goals, for set objectives and accomplishing them develops the character of discipline.

The character of Discipline therefore is continuity or habitual actions done to accomplish a specific task, which is the foundation for the development of Management skills.

The challenge this personality has is adapting to change. Change though is constant, and in a business environment both internally and externally there is continuous change. This requires creativity and innovation from the business to survive and be successful in the element of change.

We will further discuss how this personality can easily adopt the ability to accept change

### The Hare – The Hustler

The Hare is a mammal that looks similar to a rabbit. It is much larger though and has long powerful hind legs that make them fast runners. They have many predators, to which they use their speed and diligence to evade and not get caught.

In folklores the Hare is depicted as a personality of intuition, inspiration, ambitious, creative, crafty and swift. These characteristics are the foundational thought of a Hustler, the personality that wishes to get things done and in a quick time.

This personality identifies readily available resources and employs them to accomplish goals and objectives. As previously highlighted the Hare has developed speed and skill to escape predators, a Hustler usually exercises its strength to evade a situation or use its advantage in resources in making good an available opportunity.

Because of the energy exhausted in speed, creativity and inspiration the Hare do tire and often needs to rest for the sake of recuperation and renewal. The same for a Hustler, which cannot sustain energy of speed on long term business objectives as such they prefer to have short term goals with maximum results.

With the attribute of intuition, the Hare is forward thinking, it has learned and understands the environment in which it has to exist and exercises that knowledge so as to escape its predators. The Hustler exhibits this skill by ensuring it is well networked and resourceful, so it can employ strategic (outside the box) thinking to ensure its goals are achieved.

The Hare being chased has swift reflexes which allow it to easily adapt to changes in direction and make the necessary adjustment to continue its escape. With this characteristic the Hare successfully evades predators. Like the Hare in having swift reflexes, the Hustler often practices 'leaps of faith' or 'changes in direction' often challenging itself in new ventures and business initiatives.

The challenge with this personality is the ability to apply process, policies and practices to accomplish long term goals. This personality finds it difficult in upholding maintenance and accountability measures.

## The Race – The Business Journey

A race is a 'timed event, measuring speed at a predetermined distance.' The Tortoise and the Hare both agreed to engage in a race.

The Hare had all the resources to finish the race **first** as the objective. **To finish first** requires speed and agility.

The Tortoise did not have the resources to finish the race first, but he had the resources to **complete the predetermined distance** as his objective.

***The Hare can finish the race first while the Tortoise can complete the predetermined distance. Note the difference.***

The Business Journey like the Race is looked at differently by the Hustler (Hare) and the Manager (Tortoise).

The Hustler sees goals and objectives based on his needs, readily available opportunities and timeliness. It employs its talent and all available resources to ensure the objective is accomplished in the quickest time possible. Time is a motivating factor for the Hustler, as it always holds its business objective before it and will 'change direction' (leap of faith) to have its goal achieved in the shortest time possible if faced with the challenges of the business journey environment. "Time is of the essence" for the Hustler.

The Manager personality sees the course like the tortoise, as a predetermined distance to be completed at its own pace.

The Manager personality will instill practices and processes with accountability measures to ensure objectives and goals are achieved.

Time and outside influences are not a major factor for the Manager; as such the Manager may not be forward thinking or readily includes 'change of direction' actions to successfully navigate the challenges the business journey environment presents that may prevent an objective or goal from being achieved timely.

The application of both the Hustler and the Manager personalities are important to the success of any business journey.

Having knowledge and understanding of the different phases the business journey experiences, can lend guidance to the business owner on when to apply the Manager and Hustler skill sets.

Let us take a quick look at the different stages of the business journey.

## Business Journey - Phases

The Race in the Fable has a predetermined distance. A journey is similar as it also has a predetermined distance.

When one embarks on a physical journey they have to be familiar with the terrain and the distance to be travelled. They use support systems of compasses, maps and environmental tools to guide them along their journey. Often landmarks are used to measure the progress of the journey.

It is the same with a business journey as there must be an objective to be achieved and milestones or transitions/phases to measure the success of the actions taken. One must use the support systems to facilitate the ease of passage and to traverse the unexpected in the business environment.

Therefore all businesses must have a Business Plan. The Business Plan is the written plan that highlights the objectives and goals for the business in a specific time frame. At each phase of the Business Life Cycle a Plan should be developed and actioned to ensure the business is successful in its operations at that phase of its journey.

The Business Plan will lay out the resources, process and timelines to accomplish the set objectives and goals for that period.

The different phases of the business journey require the owner to implement different strategies and the utilization of diverse skill sets at each phase. The adoption of the right process at the right time will bring about the desired results for continued growth and development.

The distinct phases are:

- Trust
- Self Sufficiency
- Innovation and Action
- Enterprising
- Distinction
- Cohesiveness
- Commitment
- Continuity

## Trust

The business must initially build trust. Trust here speaks to both Internal and External trust. This will be:

- Bookkeeping Practices
- Understanding and operating in the uniqueness of your service
- Consumer Confidence
- Financial Institution Comfort
- Investor Confidence
- Supplier Trust

The first stage of Trust is important to the business and the skills of the Manager in application of bookkeeping, administration and accountability is crucial. Establishing simple administration processes and transaction recording practices will be necessary by the Manager personality.

The skill of the Hustler to build the relationship network system for the business at this phase is important. The Hustler will be needed for the Marketing and Consumer outreach. Attracting the right investors, negotiating with suppliers and building employee loyalty will require the skill set of the Hustler.

## Self-Sufficiency

Once the Owner was effective in the first phase, the business will easily experience the next phase of self-sufficiency. At this stage building internal resources is required. This will include additional sources of income (passive income), the right human capital (knowledge capital), acquisition of plant and equipment, property etc. The skills of negotiating and networking are important in this phase which is easily expressed by the Hustler. In this phase financial management, risk management and human resource management can be easily achieved via the Manager temperament.

## Innovation and Action

The business having built trust and self-sufficiency is poised to improve on its services and products through innovation. These innovative strategies require creativity and intuition. The Hustler being well networked and outgoing will have market knowledge, competitor information and industry insight to support what the business needs to successfully complete this phase of the business journey. The business having a strong management profile from being self-sufficient will have the necessary institution knowledge, management and supervisory skills and healthy financial management to venture into innovation for the continued growth of the business.

## Enterprising

At this phase, the business will have established a stable network, secure financial income streams and sturdy management practices and processes. The business can implement enterprising protocol, where the aim of this phase is to gain market share, mass marketing and production. This is the expansion stage. The Hustler personality of marketing and negotiating is important for this stage while the Manager skill set is needed for risk management, bookkeeping and internal operations expansion.

## Distinction

After gaining much market share and having secure and strong business operation ethics, it is ideal for the business to begin to be distinctive. After many years of market experience and exposure, the business can safely tend to distinguish itself in the market and against its competitors. This phase will be successful based on the network that was created for the business by the Hustler and the business culture image that was created by the Manager. It is where the Hustler and Manger true ideals are highlighted and the evidence of the governance principles that are being exercised along the company's business journey.

## Cohesiveness

With the prior phases of expansion and distinction of the business much emphasis was placed on external outreach, which is the Hustler comfort zone. This phase will require looking internally, where there will be more staff and increase work. The Manager personality focusing on institution knowledge, financial management, human resource management and administration will apply policies, practices and processes to stabilize the business and prepare it for sustainability and continued growth. The Hustler should emphasize on the Corporate Social Responsibility image of the business by trying to enhance and make better to the public opinion and grow internal brand loyalty.

## Commitment

At this phase the leaders of the business would have created a stable entity after experiencing the various stages of the business journey. They need to at this time review the business eco-system, ensuring the business has met its objectives and is resourced for its next phase. The Hustler personality in the presence of the business has the opportunity to ensuring the business is learned and understands the environment it exists in. The Manager is employed to crystallize institutional knowledge and emphasize business culture.

# Continuity

This continuity season of the business embraces the need to instill long term practices of habitual application of creativity, discipline, management practices, negotiating skills, networking, accountability measures and strategy that will realize the business longevity and success.

Improving systems, adapting to industry trends, and employing new applications are measures to ensure the business remains viable and functional in the changes that occur in the environment.

This is the point where the owners consider waste management through staff restructuring, change of or additional plant and machinery, property, operating technology and institution knowledge application.

The business may see it fit to learn efficiency in operations and improve in its leadership accountability by solidify training in leadership to its managers and institutional knowledge to its team to ensure the business can be successful in legacy building.

## Story Analysis

Understanding the events in the story and how they occurred will help us have a clear idea on seeing the strengths and the weaknesses of each of the animals.

### The Callout

Let us examine the Hare's Introduction to the Tortoise.

> '"A Hare was making fun of the Tortoise one day for being so slow. "Do you ever get anywhere?" he asked with a mocking laugh."'

The Hare knowing his strength in being fast was comfortable in making fun at the Tortoise for being slow. Again it can be noted here that time is of the essence for the Hare. His mocking laugh to the Tortoise highlights that the Hare prioritize quick completion of any journey.

The Hustler also portrays this energy in wanting quick completion, to the business objective, sometimes evading mandatory obligations, rules or regulations. It is difficult for the Hustler to adopt practices, processes, institutional knowledge and policies in the completion of a goal or objective.

The Hare like the Hustler exhibits energy of confidence and self-expression. They are sociable and outgoing challenging the status quo can be listed as one of their traits. The Hustler is excellent in networking, marketing and sales generation. They can easily be the face of the business creating relationships that are necessary for the business to be recognized in the market. The Hustler's mind is quick and sees opportunities and challenges easily.

The Hustler is always on the go and it tends to be difficult for this energy to be burdened with management responsibilities. To help the Hustler personality in adopting the business culture one has to build accountability measures into the Hustler's expectations using short term goals.

A Hustler temperament as a Sole Trader or Micro Enterprise should outsource administrative and financial services or have internal personnel hold you accountable on the delivery of these matters. This will help establish the necessary management activities needed to support the business in sustainability and growth.

## The Response

Here we will consider the Tortoise response and what ensued.

> '"Yes," replied the Tortoise, "and I get there sooner than you think. I'll run you a race and prove it." The Hare was much amused at the idea of running a race with the Tortoise, but for the fun of the thing he agreed. So the Fox, who had consented to act as judge, marked the distance and started the runners off'.

The Tortoise responded saying "I get there sooner than you think". This statement seemed carefully thought out, for the Tortoise did not confidently tell the Hare he will be faster than him in a race, but that he (the Tortoise) can finish a race faster than what the Hare might think.

Now the Manager tends to evaluate a situation before responding. They will consider the different options and select the most appropriate to the situation. The Manager response will be presented as being a reserved and 'safe' one. This approach exercises risk management qualities and can tend to be lengthy and burdensome if left unchecked.

The Hare responded in amusement at the thought of the Tortoise in a race. He probably did not listen to the Tortoise as the Tortoise did not profess to win but to complete a race in his shortest time possible.

Nevertheless, the Hare, seeing an opportunity to invest his resource of speed and make his objective of ridiculing the Tortoise complete, agreed to running a race with the Tortoise 'for the fun of it'.

The Fox marked the distance to be attempted by the Tortoise and the Hare. The distance was the same objective for both the Tortoise and the Hare. The distance that was marked by the Fox can be likened to the main objective of a business which is to make a profit; that is as a business owner the goals set will be to ensure the business venture is a viable and profitable one. Like the tortoise and the hare, the Hustler and the Manager personalities both have the same objective on their business journey.

A Hustler always looks for an opportunity to invest its resources to achieve quick profitability while the Manager sets processes and accountability measures to acquire the business goal.

## Ready, Set, Go!

'The Hare was soon far out of sight, and to make the Tortoise feel very deeply how ridiculous it was for him to try a race with a Hare, he lay down beside the course to take a nap until the Tortoise should catch up.'

And they were off! In the business journey having the right resources and inspiration or an innovative entrepreneurial energy is important, it gets you started.

The Hare using his resource of speed; applied it excellently (Inspiration) and was well ahead of the Tortoise. The Hustler also tends to function solo. This means he/she do not burden themselves with responsibilities, like the shell of the Tortoise, which may hinder the objective of achieving their goal timely.

One of the Hustler's motivations is competition. In a competitive environment the Hustler will perform at its best. It will exhaust its energy and other means to be better than the others. Its yardstick for performance is the performance of others. If the

Hustler is not aware of any competition, it may not create a yardstick.

The Hare's objective was not to finish the race first but to prove the Tortoise that he was a slow animal. The Hare like the Hustler can be distracted from completing the main objective of the journey.

Because the Hare made the Tortoise the competition when he saw he had quite a distance between him and the Tortoise he decided to stop running and take a nap.

This action on the business journey is extremely dangerous. Asleep here for the Hustler can be described as having a lack of knowledge, getting complacent in utilizing its resources and not applying the necessary management skills.

The Hustler desires quick / immediate success for its business objective therefore it tires easily if the process becomes tardy for completion, often times abandoning one project to start another.

A hustler must develop the habit of having a steady objective or goal in mind that is predetermined on the long term success of the business, while recognizing achievements or milestones on its business journey.

If the Hare had done this, his objective would have been to finish the race, instead he saw the need to prove his speed, ridicule the Tortoise and rest.

'The Tortoise meanwhile kept going slowly but steadily, and, after a time, passed the place where the Hare was sleeping.'

We see the Tortoise understanding his resource of endurance, attempting the course slowly and steadily. The Tortoise's shell, which can be likened to the responsibilities a Manager embraces, can be a challenge for the Tortoise to move faster. It is therefore noteworthy that for a Manager personality to function time efficiently, the shedding of responsibilities to other capable members of the team is crucial.

The Manager personality often times find difficulty in relinquishing duties that will allow it to adopt new habits of resourcing, networking and strategy to help it survive in a business environment of constant change.

The Manager, however to remain engaged, must implement processes and procedures with accountability measures to ensure the little wins are achieved.

The Tortoise eventually passed the place where the Hare was sleeping. The Tortoise's commitment to finishing the journey was his objective. He simply continued steadily to the finishing line.

## The Finish

'But the Hare slept on very peacefully; and when at last he did wake up, the Tortoise was near the goal. The Hare now ran his swiftest, but he could not overtake the Tortoise in time.'

The finishing line was in sight, the Tortoise gradually inched to accomplishing his objective of completing the predetermined distance. The Hare, who was asleep, was awakened to the sight of the Tortoise very close to the finishing line. The Hare panicked and immediately sets about on maximizing on his resource of speed, to reach the finishing line before the Tortoise.

But alas the Tortoise was able to complete the race first.

As a business owner setting one's objective must be determined by its resources, the proper application of those resources and its mission.

If the business vision is focused on being better than the competition, their operations can be self-sabotaging. The application of resources and operations will only seek to dominate the competition. When achieved, the business which is displaying a personality of a Hustler, like the Hare may become relaxed and may not employ other opportunities, like transformational strategies to ensure the business can truly be successful in the market.

The Tortoise can be likened to the business that completed its mission. This was done as the Tortoise vision was not on the performance of the Hare but on completing the predetermined distance. When the Tortoise passed the sleeping Hare he did not stop his progress, he continued steadily. The Tortoise like the Manager is steady in its approach to achieving its objectives. It practices institutional knowledge, process application and accountability.

The application of the Hustler and Manager personalities, are both crucial for the success of the business in achieving its best.

## Summary

A predetermined distance was agreed on by two different animals that had different types of resources to accomplish the objective of completing the course in the shortest possible time.

Firstly as the owner of a business, (self-employed, sole trader or limited liability) you must first know what the mission of the business is, the predetermined distance to be accomplished. This will help the owner create visions that are focused on completing the mission of the business.

The visions should focus on the transitions period the business will experience, product life cycle, operational and transformational strategies and recovery processes. These are the different landmarks that a business will experience on its business journey. The successful achievement of the phases helps the business to be sustained, grow and gain longevity.

Both animals had different resources, very much like business in operations. The resources of businesses include their network, physical assets, institutional knowledge and culture. How these resources are applied will determine the success of completing the objectives of the business.

The use of Inspiration to the business resources will guide the business in being innovative, networking, marketing and strategic. As a business owner and leader the adoption of the skill of Inspiration helps one to:

- Establish a strong presence in its eco-system
- Understand the environment the business operates in
- Establish strong market presence; internal and external brand loyalty
- Lead in Transformational Strategies.

The use of Discipline applied to the business resources supports the business in stability, consistency and security. This environment of discipline guides the business to achieve:

- Creating a culture that supports the success of the business
- Established institutional policies and knowledge
- Continuous accountability practices
- Strong Financial and risk management position

The continued application of both Inspiration and Discipline in the activities of the business will realize the success of the business in both its internal and external environments.

Understanding your skill resource as an owner you will know what your strengths are and what you need to improve on or gain knowledge of so your business will not be lacking the important energies for it to be successful.

Consider the list of the qualities listed below for each of the personalities. Identify your strength and weaknesses and readily employ the necessary steps to ensure your business is well equipped for its journey.

The Manager will easily exhibit qualities:

- Process Oriented
- Accountability
- Analytical
- Consistency
- Planning

The Hustler will comfortably display qualities:

- Sociable
- Adaptive
- Time Efficient
- Opportunistic
- Result Oriented

As an owner it is good to operate efficiently in your strengths, but one must resource the additional energies to ensure the success of your business venture.

Having the right support then is crucial ensuring that all the skills required for the business is made available from the personnel involved in its operations.

See the Business Essence Matrix which gives a quick overview on how these skills benefit the business.

**Business Essence Matrix**

|  | HIGH — MANAGER — LOW |  |
|---|---|---|
| **HIGH** (HUSTLER) | The business is equipped to dominate the market by being well networked and establishing strong operations. | The business is well networked and marketed but may have poor operations which can lead to losses and waste of resources. |
| **LOW** | The business is well established in its operations but may not have a strong presence in the market. | The business is not well networked or marketed and it has not established stable operations. |

A business journey is an exciting and rewarding one. A business owner can look forward to the personal growth and business transformations. It is not a journey for the swiftest but for the one who exercises diligence and time efficiency.

www.ingramcontent.com/pod-product-compliance
Lightning Source LLC
Chambersburg PA
CBHW030040230526
**45472CB00002B/598**